Prayer Can Be Anything

poems by

Karen Elizabeth Sharpe

Finishing Line Press
Georgetown, Kentucky

Prayer Can Be Anything

For all who believe

Copyright © 2023 by Karen Elizabeth Sharpe
ISBN 979-8-88838-286-8 First Edition
All rights reserved under International and Pan-American Copyright Conventions. No part of this book may be reproduced in any manner whatsoever without written permission from the publisher, except in the case of brief quotations embodied in critical articles and reviews.

ACKNOWLEDGMENTS

Grateful acknowledgement is made to the following publications in which these poems first appeared, sometimes in different versions.

"A Necessary Roughness": *Columbia Journal*
"A Vestigial Sense": *Split Rock Review*
"Exhalation": *West Trade Review*
"How to Know Hunger Like the Kingfisher": *The Hard Word of Hope*
"How I Shoplift": *Mom Egg Review*
"My Old Dog Speaks": *Verse Virtual*
"Nucleation of the Wood Frog": *Mason Street Review*
"The Balance in Question": *Poetry Sunday*
"The Surety of This Late Winter Light": *Mizmour Anthology*
"When I Finally Take the Antidepressants": *Intima Journal*

Publisher: Leah Huete de Maines
Editor: Christen Kincaid
Cover Art: "Little Pine Sunset" by Lauren Rutten
Author Photo: Devin Rae Hart
Cover Design: Elizabeth Maines McCleavy

Order online: www.finishinglinepress.com
also available on amazon.com

Author inquiries and mail orders:
Finishing Line Press
PO Box 1626
Georgetown, Kentucky 40324
USA

Table of Contents

We Begin in Wetness 1
In Which I Storytell You Into Something I Can't Say 2
On My Twelfth Birthday 3
Going to School after Your Father Dies 4
Everything, I am Safe Here 5
In the Shadow of Leviticus 6
This Poem Wants to be a Love Poem So Bad 7
Exhalation 8
Moon as Witness 9
The Art of Harvesting 13
A Necessary Roughness 14
How to Know Hunger like the Kingfisher 15
Nucleation of the Wood Frog 16
Sticks, then Stones 17
Sleeping Dogs 18
Field Notes for my Ex-Husband 19
My Old Dog Speaks 20
In Tennessee I Contemplate 23
Firmament's Crack 24
When I Finally Take the Antidepressants 25
Ode on Gluttony 26
A Vestigial Sense 27
When Marriage Calls Love after the Breakup 28
Plate Tectonics 29
Reflections on Sex Lessons 30
How I Shoplift 31
October, the Last Month Before We Separated 32
The Balance in Question 33
The Surety of This Late Winter Light 34

I

We Begin in Wetness

I knew my mother like this once:
    she was an ocean, drifting
        I was her erosion, her brimming.

In her body's warm bowl of beginnings
    I was her dream-soaked awakening.
        I was the strength of her shins

the shifting tide of her thighs
    I shone like the silver moon reflecting
        the basin of my mother's bellying

in her beginnings.
    In her bowl of tangy brine
        I braved her heartbreath's beating

I songed her silent wantings
    talked her briny rhythms
        I liquored the drink of her heat

her trust, suckled on her mistrust
    recited her thousand names.
        In the warm bowl of my mother's beginnings

I was her sand glass, her cross staff
    her sweep-and-turn, a sextant
        a lead line, a star chart.

I was her christening, her compass
    a destining, her reckoning.

In Which I Storytell You Into Something I Can't Say

Lift me up counter.
        Height my performance.
Donut rows word choke child.
        Co-co-nut-na-mon,
Honey glazed ladygirl.
        Serving coffee winks.
How are you a little lady?
        I don't answer like.
Fine, thank you.
        I say Sugarfrostfrostnot.
How are you? May I have a do-do-di-donot.
        Choc-o-frostajelly. Wannadustalicious.
Hear my. *I'm fine. Tank you. Tang.*
        Ting. Ting. Stutt. Ting. Stutting.
Ting. Hear my disap.
        A pear.
                A pear.
                      A pear.
A pear. Ring.   Sugar in water.
        Devil's cruel food cruel. Cruler. My.
My empty mouth.
        Hole. Whole. Could fall into.
Crust my sweet hole.
        World.

On My Twelfth Birthday

Taking a break from
caring for my dying father

my mother, hair cut short
something drawing her attention

beyond the party
cacophony, a dozen girls

rushing through
the house all awkward

grace, a flock
of starlings.

Her eyes how thin.
How young.

At his funeral, she stood
between my brother and me

in the receiving line
hands on our shoulders

light as wings.

Going to School after Your Father Dies

At school, if your father is dead
you're as weird as a broken moon

an igneous, crystalized
stone of a girl whose mother

is never around, maybe there's
a boy two years older than you

who lives down the street
pushing up your shirt saying

come on, come on. In your neighborhood
there are only boys. You never walk alone.

At school all the girls say *tell us
everything* knowing you won't.

In your room, on Saturdays, when no one
is around, bashed on sweet aperitifs and birdie

juice vodka punch from the liquor cabinet
you practice reciting the word deceased.

Everything, I am Safe Here

On the screen porch glider after supper
luminescent lamplight flickering my shoulders

I see myself cocooned in loons' runic calls
paper moth wings wisping screens, my grandmother

close by crosswording, her knobby fingers slipping
dictionary pages, glinting glasses orbing the light.

The moon at night is bright as an egg, the welkin sky
shimmering a sprinkle of starry salt and my father

silent, riveted steel in a paperback, tackle box
and pole stationed morning-ready, as my mother washes

dishes, all our camp plates, all our bellies full
her hands wrinkled, soapy; warm.

In the Shadow of Leviticus

And yet, what I am afraid to say
about my father

I hint at now and then
to myself, to my mother

in a conversation
she won't have.

His shadow washes the walls
trembling home movies

playing across a sheet
hung over the door to the den

lights out, his cigarette
lit up in the corner

blinking red eye.

*I don't know why
you can't remember him*

more fondly

my mother says.

This Poem Wants to be a Love Poem So Bad

Billy Idol pulls my hair into pointy blonde spikes
throws a collar on me and I'm grooving

even before my strangled voice went bankrupt.
I'm not saying my father abandoned me.

He just died, stranding me on the flip side of 13
when I was a needle ready for a vein.

I back-fill over and over in search of him.
I habit my way into a scrum of boys

dancing to the radio on the patio.
I want to be the drug of their addiction.

You look like a hooker. It's my mother
standing in our orange and yellow kitchen

phone cord twisting her fingers, you can't
go out like that, she says.

My edge already bent.

Exhalation

Chain-smoking in the backseat
I touch the fire end
to a new cigarette, inhale.

    Tracy across my lap, eyes closed.
    I tuck the cigarette in her fingers
    light another for myself.

Car windows cracked, cold air sluicing.
Up front, her boyfriend,
Jeff, grips the wheel.

    Pewter countryside sews itself
    together. Winter shivering.
    This morning we skipped school

drove to New Hampshire
with $300 cash, the clinic
two hours away.

    Below closed lids
    Tracy's eyes scan
    cigarette pluming.

At 15, neither of us could drive or get an abortion
in our state without a parent's permission.
We never thought about permission.

    Rivers of trees stream by.
    We were twigs pale and growing
    inside our dark bark.

Moon as Witness

              I was on the wane. I could hear them laughing
        drinking behind the cinder block garage wall.

        Four neighborhood boys and a girl, teenagers.
    Their eyes like strobes flashing. Laugh, flash, laugh.

    Then, the boys wrestling. Three on one
they called each other retard, other names.

  People did that then. Said things
that offended, laughing.

Moths at window lights, tapping
houses behind the wall, fireflies flashing.

She was standing, still as a fence post looking
   at me, dark skirt of the sky between us.

  One boy joking a hat on her head
     then pulling it, it was over her eyes.

      Then another tied her hands, eye strobes flashing.
        I was helpless, barely enough light to see.

        For nights after I heard the stories:
           Just Another Wrong Place and Time.

          What Was She Wearing? You Know
            She Was Drunk. Boys Will be Boys.

    Nights, years later, I hear them, still, now slanting:
She Should Be Over It By Now.   Why Bring It Up Again?   Move On.

      I wish I said something.   So much collected blue.
         I staple up my rotten sky night

           after night with my own me toos.

II

The Art of Harvesting

Be careless of nothing.
Enter the woods in silence.
Follow the scat, tracks, and scrapes.

Whitetail ears tune like turrets
to any stitch of sound, nose
stronger than bloodhound.

Camouflage downwind, a coverscent
cologne and rubber boots, dusted with dirt.
Blaze the treestand orange and pine.

Wait. Pockets stuffed
with handwarmers. Nothing ends
a hunt faster than shivering.

Practice fern yellow, moss green.
Practice stillness, shallow breathing.
Once you see him gliding in the wood

his silken eye, his walnut hide
finger-tight your trigger squeeze
smoke the forest with the scent of blood.

Vacate your heart of sound. Praise
the flank, the rack of eight.
Name him good. Name him food.

A Necessary Roughness

Some argue a knife behind the head
straight through the spine is the most humane

but I learned the killing of fish
begins with a hard whack from the hammer

the clean dispatch of a blunt tool
some call the priest

direct and firm to the skull
where there can be no irony

in the blessing of submission
just a necessary roughness

and tension as the shock stuns
a bloody bloom on the stilled canvas

as the knife slips in.

How to Know Hunger like the Kingfisher

Make yourself
high on a perch

plunge headfirst
below muscled waves.

a plummet of halcyon gash
and dagger-shaped bill.

30 feet or more. Pluck the silver
slipper craving of fish.

Fan your wings and rise.
High on a snag of hemlock

pound it bloody red.
There's nothing

to fear or regret.
Swallow headfirst.
Whole.

Nucleation of the Wood Frog

In winter, the wood frog freezes solid
beside the pond, buried in leaf litter.

Crystalized skin and muscle.
Heart stills. Lungs shut down.

Organs dehydrate in the frog's own sweet
antifreeze. Pupils rime over.

Then, a biological miracle, the frog
thaws from the inside out.

Warm light emanating from within.
Heart beats. Brain activates.

Legs move in search for love immediate:
eggs, sperm, tadpole into another life.

When I was a girl I adored
the wood frog's song. To hide in mud.

Behind trees. I learned to trust the shadow
beneath the fern, the places outside my father's house.

When I was a girl, I'd be like the wood frog
when my father strapped me with his belt.

Now, at night, I can lie still and quiet
a certain, unfrozen heart.

Sticks, then Stones

I began kicking the dog
kneeing her brown and white flank

hurting like the dickens, like the devil
my grandmother said

because I needed
someone new to beat on

once my little brother got too big
once he learned to kick back

heels to haunches, fists to ribs
sticks and stones, a world of hurt

as in, you've got to love
like you've never been hurt

as in, we only hurt the ones we love
as in, this hurts like hell

as in, oh, cry me a river
as in, hurt people hurt

people. Who cared back then?
Spilt milk? No one tried.

Wolf? No one cried.
I thought it wouldn't hurt a bit

but it's the truth
that haunts the most.

The dog took it all, every time.
loyal as only love could be.

Sleeping Dogs

That December
my husband's cancer
was the one declared
in remission. Not our old dog's.
Too cold for another dog,
he warned me.

I couldn't stand the quiet.
Her empty collar tucked
into the bookcase, water
bowl under the sink.
I began pacing our woods
getting lost, counting days.

In April, my husband relented.
The new dog busted up
our expectations. No shoes
un-chewed. No lawn un-dug.
Still, the stony field
of silence between us.

Each night, by the blue light
of the television, I sagged
into a chair, my husband
and the new dog couched together:
their evening news, their feet tangled
and touching, their anxious twitching.

Field Notes for my Ex-Husband

I seeded the porch steps
    with distraction,

black sunflower constellations
    laced with wheat.

You thistled feeders on the decking rail.
    I watched from inside as

tananger and rubythroats savored
    orange on a stick.

Birders call the ongoing tally
    of species sightings a life list.

I kept a tally of us too:
    a betrayal of common jay

grievance of goldfinch on the wing
    cardinal's gaslit ghost-flame.

The silence of barbed bristle-feathers
    around the mouth.

Bird by bird we catalogued the end
    of desire, of frivolity, of flight.

We didn't say who was right
    or who was wrong

when we set our field glasses down.

My Old Dog Speaks

Each day you leave me.
I have come to expect it

and do not suffer. By now
we wear each other

like an old pair of slippers
and besides, I am tired.

For 13 years I have held my tongue
except when the crows get raucous

in the field out back, yet now
I must tell you: There is nothing

to be afraid of. When I close my eyes
after you go to work, when I lay down

and my bones click into place
the field is all around me

lit with daisies and purple
clover full of bees.

Each day you leave me I see
more clearly the jays and sparrows

the places where dreams go
the stories you'll tell

the golden sunlight, forgiving
and going on forever.

III

In Tennessee I Contemplate

When I hit a town called Bucksnort
Hank jangles on the radio
You're gonna change your way of livin'
Change the things you do.

Semis double up on Highway 40.
Lank dank stretchiness of road.
Stop doin' all them things
that you hurtin' to.

98 burning degrees outside.
I'm tired of shoveling the ocean.
Your daddy's mad, he's done got peeved
You gonna change or I'm a-gonna leave.

Love feels like a razor
I pull dull my own pain with.
You gonna change
or I'm gonna leave.

Love's a sweet glue like paste.
Moons for sale for someone else.
A nightlong skittered dopamine
starring my eastern skies pink.

What wastes in me listens.

Firmament's Crack

Frost fissures erupt
across the field.

Sod turns itself over
a cheerless earth.

But the firecracker
zinnias keep blooming.

Head in the stars. Pain
is the best kind of invisible.

When frost takes the rest
of the garden down to dead

I cover it in leaf mulch
as if this year is the same

as any other.

When I Finally Take the Antidepressants

I read the label on the bottle
and sound it out: Esci-tal-o-pram.

I want it to say *Escape it Again.*
Exit to Siam. Eggs Tukmenistan.

I take my antidepressants like punishment.
I stand in the corner. I'm in time out.

I want to spit them out. Wash my mouth
out with soap. I want to row

away in the difficult ship of my brain
drink herbal concoctions

become devout, pray with a shaman
get stuck with needles to cleanse

my cloudy aura. Escape it again.
Malediction of promise.

I want to talk about
this anchor of sadness: my tedious

metaphor about my sinking boat.
I want to talk to my therapist

tell her I'm going to try again.
I'll take two and call her in the morning.

I'm willing to trust her gravity.

Ode on Gluttony

Beautiful giant, mother of all sins
you swallow me whole
your wanton plumpness.
I slip you on so simply I could cry.
You nourish my spare and skinny heart
like a tray of lasagna
no one else in the room.

You are kinder and more saccharine
than my mother's endless chatter.
Your effortless comfort fills my ear
better than lunchroom gossip
better than my fanciful faked orgasm
groaned for everyone else but me.
You're more evil delight than a cat
menacing a golden chipmunk.

Throat of throats
I am a crime scene in your presence.
You are my binge of Law & Order
all Saturday afternoon.
With you, I never get out of my pajamas.
You're my confidante, my consort
my endless glass of wine.

Let's change our names
Bread & Butter, Cheese & Crackers
let's run away together, let's get married
bake an enormous cake, angel food
a mountain of sweetness
we can get lost in.

A Vestigial Sense

> *Majority of Kids Would Rather Lose Their Sense of Smell Than Lose Facebook* —Headline in PC Magazine

Do they think smell
is the province of lesser animals
pigs rooting out truffles
sharks scenting blood
dogs olfactory tracking at a park?

We have spent centuries writing
off Plato's *half formed* and Kant's
most disposable sense
as less than, feeble, insignificant
a vestigial way of knowing, a witchcraft.

Imagine, just as a side effect
of breathing, knowing
this blue sweater has been worn
and this white one hasn't.

That the petrichored blood of stones
now rising from fresh rain
will tender the lawnmower
perfume of grass and gasoline.

How a sunset alchemized afternoon
can elicit your savory chicken
its sweet and tangy sauce
charring on the grill.

And this too,
how even blindfolded
recognizing the fragrance
that love once wore.

When Marriage Calls Love after the Breakup

The week after I kicked you out of the house
I realize I don't really like being alone. I want
to tell you I'm sorry for kicking you out but I'm mixed up.
I'm so used to Love's drug I can't help myself. So I call.

You pick up right away like you've been waiting for me.
You say, hey Marriage, I'm better. I'm going to counseling.
It's like learning French. You say the French word for what we said
to each other is *promesses*, which means till the end of time.

You are getting so much out of counseling. You blame
your lack of mother love for your anger issues. You say
I have love issues but you get me now. We're *meilleur ou pire*, right?
You say, Marriage, trust me, Love can make anything happen.

I say, Love, how come you never wanted counseling before?
What we said to each other was a warm throat pink and torn
a stone thrown down, was soap opera.
You say, Marriage, we said till death do us part.

You say I should let you back in.
Love's always charming my promises into astonishment.
You say, only we can control our own feelings.
You say, Marriage, I know you better than you know yourself.

I remember you used to watch Jeopardy every night
pay attention like a dog on a squirrel to everything but me.
I never asked to read your texts—those are private—
why you hate holding hands or public displays of affection.

So now when I say what was with the Jamieson bottle
under the Honda's front seat and the swinger shit on the computer?
All you say is c'mon, Marriage, we promised, no matter what
this is wedlock. I tell Love what I give and get back
in return never weighs the same.

Plate Tectonics

For my ex-husband

How precise the word fault is.

Your ruptured point, my weakness.
A break in continuity, a dislocation.

A slagged slab split, a breach, a buckle
and trench, no longer continent, or ocean,

an indelicate tremble and subduction
of across, transverse, over and against.

It's been two years since I called
your bluff about breaking up, called

our rift of trust too much,
our strike-slip, our side-to-side,

collision displaced, a continental
drift, called our marriage over,

the divergent boundaries
of your idea of love

and my idea of love
pushing apart

new sea floor emerging.

Reflections on Sex Lessons

I aimed to be
loved, or at least necessary.
I didn't know
I could say no.
Pointed at my body:
This old thing? Just slipped it on.
Later, I said no
but my voice was only inside.
I had studied at the school
of the encrypted. Father's
teasing, nameless women,
Penthouses, Playboys
under the beds, crumpled.
Mother's slim magazine lessons
dictating: stay skinny
keep your man happy
dinner in 30 minutes or less.

Dinner in 30 minutes. Or less
keeping your man happy.
Dictating: stay skinny
mothers. Slim magazine lessons
under the beds. Crumpled
Penthouses, Playboys
teasing. Nameless women
of the encrypted fathers.
I had studied at the school
but my voice was only inside.
Later, I said no.
This old thing. Just slipped it on,
pointed at my body.
I could say, No,
I didn't know.
Loved, or at least necessary
I aimed to be.

How I Shoplift

I check out invisibly.
Isolation rides invisibly
in the child's seat of my
cart heart.

I want my life back.
Even if I have to steal it.
I swipe one, take two:
Clorox, toothpaste, crosswords,
tape—not Scotch—a knock-off brand
to piece together scraps
of Addonizio's *What is this thing called love*
that my new shelter dog chewed up
because she got off the transport
van from North Carolina shivering
and chewing the way an addict
follows a familiar route of loneliness.

I refund myself in sweet potatoes
debit life of this pandemic
payback for time lost
for the grinding of my teeth at night
a cake for the birthday my daughter
had to celebrate alone.

Sunflower seeds, striped ones
for bluejays crowding my deck
bluejays which symbolize clear vision
or endurance, or safety, or protection
depending on which spirit guide
I google that day.

A bathing suit, sunblock
watermelon for the summer I missed
each skipped scanner
swipe at the checkout
sweet soundless restitution.

October, the Last Month Before We Separated

We held each other at a distance
but sometimes not.

You'd wanted to hold on to me with pliers
rather than open the shell of your ear.

Feelings, you said,
can be forgotten.

In the garden the cosmos
bloomed red, magenta, and pink.

I had to stop myself from going to look
at their joyous illusion.

And then the last weekend
we pulled off the greatest farce of all

going to the wedding of the son of a friend
in the Blue Ridge Mountains

On the morning of the ceremony
I thought of us unwedding

then climbed the Humpback Ridge
to look out over the sprawling

Afton Valley, suddenly eager.

The Balance in Question

Last night, the crescent of new moon
clawed at the western sky.
Coyotes yowled at the wind.

In morning, daylight silvers
maple sap pails, spigots,
tubing strung along the road.

I'm alone again. My balance
in question, my spring
a wand of light warmed

by window glass, winter
a scab of snow in the field.
Fullness swells fingers of hyacinth

robins camouflage among
sumac berries. The pileated's rumble
hammers a hole big as a fist in my heart.

The Surety of This Late Winter Light

Prayer can be a pile
of roadside stones, beseeching.

The quicksand sorrow invokes.
The hemlock across the lake,

supplicant in thin-needled halo light.
It doesn't have to be

text, wafer, or baptism,
two hands pressed, rosary clicking.

Witness silver morning light
polish the empyrean sky,

the great blue heron
keyholing the elaborate blue,

the near perfect rumor
of waning snow,

the surety of this late winter light,
however stretched and thin.

www.ingramcontent.com/pod-product-compliance
Lightning Source LLC
Chambersburg PA
CBHW022123090426
42743CB00008B/981